AF879427

Dollar Happy Workbook

Copyright © 2021 Dora DeLellis, CPA, MST, CFP®

ISBN: 978-0-9974244-6-1

When is financial satisfaction achieved?
When you have the following:

- A manageable debt level
- A spending plan
- Ability to handle large ticket purchases
- An emergency fund
- No money discord
- No money secrets
- Low money stress
- A realistic plan

Contrary to what you see on Facebook and Instagram, financial satisfaction is not when you live in mansion on a cliff overlooking the ocean. It's not when you own the latest cool thing. It's when you have a money plan that allows you to meet your monthly financial obligations and you can work toward building wealth. It's about being at peace with your finances where you don't have to lie to others or yourself about what you have or don't have. It's about having an earning plan and a spending plan.

Make sure to celebrate the small efforts. Focus on what you have done and why it worked. Then do it again.

Where are you on the Money Behavior Spectrum?

What can you do to create more balance?

Money decisions are controlled by money beliefs. Your financial mindset, or money script, is responsible for what goes right or wrong in your money life. Because money scripts propel actions, they deserve acknowledgement and recognition. Money scripts are based on unconscious beliefs and can be tough to uncover – it requires deep thinking and self reflection to jiggle these views from the brain tunnels where they're nestled. Some are good, some are bad. Recognizing false beliefs and irrational judgements requires a mature attitude adjustment.

To better understand your money script, read:

"Mind Over Money"
by Dr. Brad Klontz

Money Jar

fill in the blanks

Financial Visions

Financial Visions

The Business

	JAN	FEB	MAR	APR	MAY	JUN
REVENUE						
Income						
LESS EXPENSES						
Rent/Mortgage						
Car Payment						
Groceries						
Car Insurance						
Health Insurance						
Electric						
Phone						
Cable						
Gas						
Credit Card						
Student Loan						
Vet						
Misc.						
PROFIT						
$						

# of YOU

	JUL	AUG	SEPT	OCT	NOV	DEC
REVENUE						
Income						
LESS EXPENSES						
Rent/Mortgage						
Car Payment						
Groceries						
Car Insurance						
Health Insurance						
Electric						
Phone						
Cable						
Gas						
Credit Card						
Student Loan						
Vet						
Misc.						
PROFIT						
$						

Calculate Your Net Worth

ASSETS - monetary accounts and property owned

TOTAL ASSETS	

Liabilities - loans, mortgages, debt

TOTAL LIABILITIES	

NET WORTH	

Debt Paydown

Beginning Balance

$ __________

$ __________

$ __________

$ __________

$ __________

$ __________

$ __________

$ __________

$ __________

$ __________

$ __________

$ __________

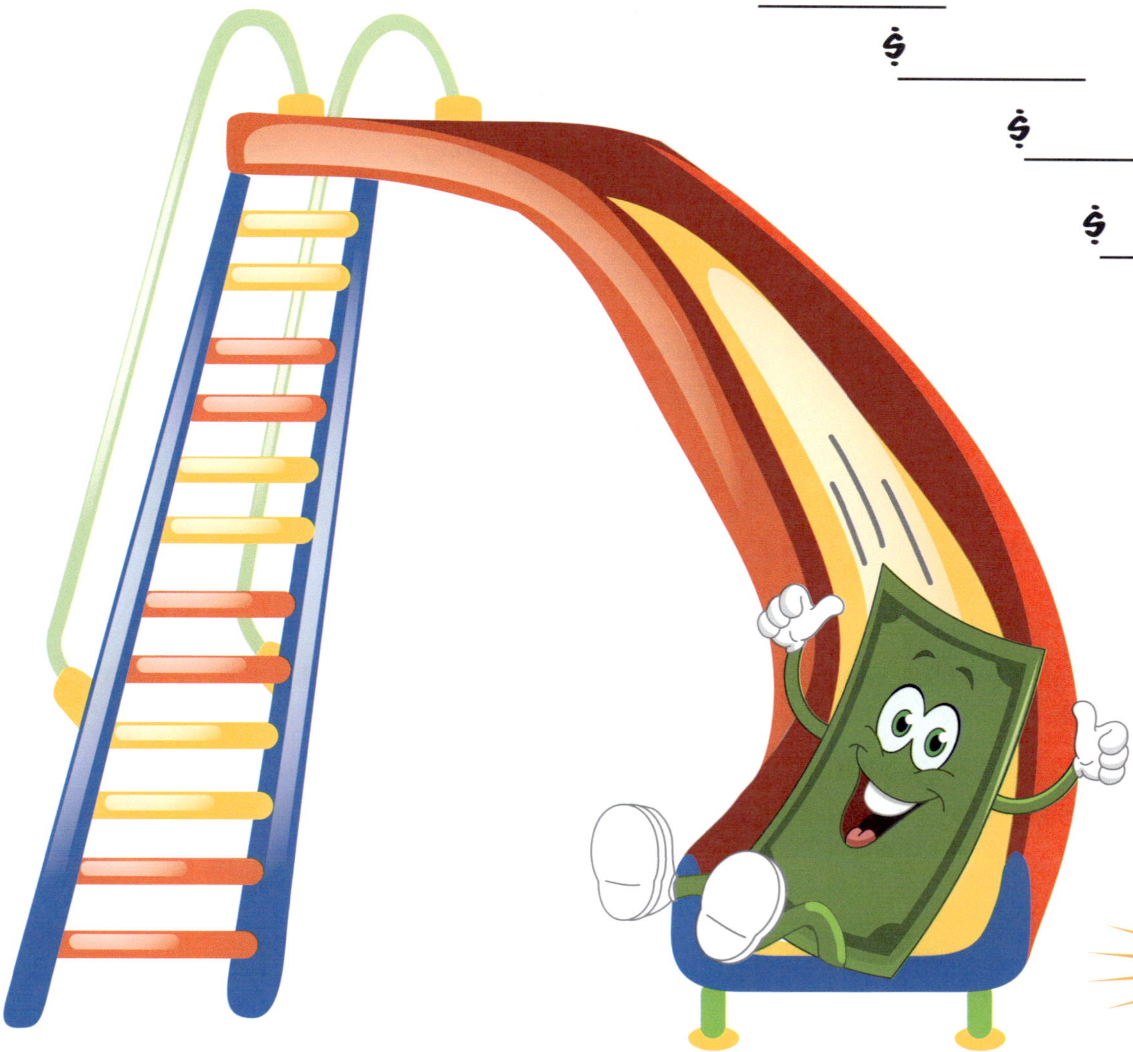

$0

Midyear Financial Checklist

- ☐ Retrieve monthly account statements. Analyze activity.
- ☐ Are my retirement account contributions high enough?
- ☐ How much money have I saved this year?
- ☐ Do I need to automate my savings or investment savings?
- ☐ Have I contributed enough to my IRAs?
- ☐ Is my money in the right accounts to reach my goals?
- ☐ How much have I invested?
- ☐ Have I contributed enough to 529 plans?
- ☐ How can I adjust insurance premiums? Suggestion: take a defensive driving class for a reduction in vehicle insurance premiums.

Extra Credit Activities:

- ☐ Think about needed big ticket purchases. Think Black Friday.
- ☐ Plan spending for off-season purchases.
- ☐ Start your own holiday fund. Suggestion: purchase a gift card each month and save them for holiday purchases.
- ☐ Set up a tax return folder. Is income tax withholding adequate? Too much or too little should be adjusted now.
- ☐ Reward yourself for taking care of this now, not burdening yourself with all of it at holiday time.

Celebrate your successes!

Notes

CHALLENGE

Determine Wants vs. Needs

Wants	Needs

Fill in the Pie

Where do your monthly profits go?

- Savings
- College Fund
- Investments
- Other

Create a spending plan and list 5 alternatives to spending:

Expense	When

Alternatives to Spending

Ex: Exercise

YOURSELF

What are some things your money script leads you to do? How can you alter extreme behaviors?

Behaviors

Remedies

List Small Successes Here:

List your money fears and decide how you will overcome them.

Think...

How are you valuing your time?

MORE

Organize all of your insurance policies. Determine if your insurance coverage is adequate. How can you reduce your premiums?

Ideas:

How can you convert your earned income into passive income?

How are you making your money work for you?

More

Ideas to increase your net worth:

CHALLENGES

Use the Yahoo Finance Stock Screener to choose 3 new companies to invest in.

Stock symbol: ______________________

Why did you choose this business to invest in?

Stock symbol: ______________________

Why did you choose this business to invest in?

Stock symbol: ______________________

Why did you choose this business to invest in?

Obtain your credit score from a free online service and come up with five ideas to increase it.

My Credit Score:

Ideas:

Thinking!

What would your "money story" tell others:

Grade yourself on being a money manager:

A B C D F

Save

Index Funds

Stocks by Sector

Enter Symbols

Healthcare

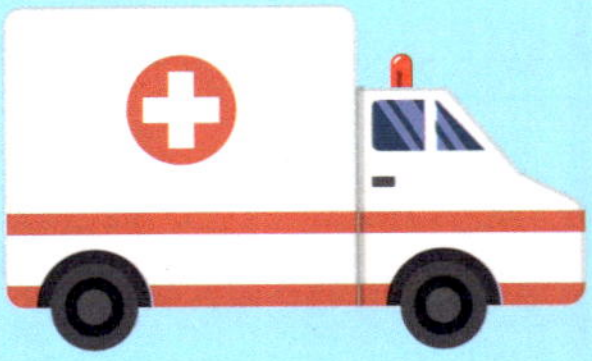

Real Estate (REITS)

Energy

Industrials

Utilities

Invest

% of Total Investments

Mutual Funds

Consumer Discretionary

Consumer Staples

Financials

Materials

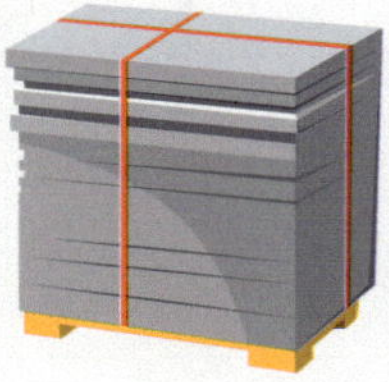

Telecommunications

Save → Invest

	Money Market/ CDs/Govt Sec	Bonds	ETFs	Preferred Stocks	Alternatives
Beginning Balance:					
TOTAL:					

Goal:					

Investing Bingo!

Create an investment allocation plan	Identify two low-risk index funds	Find the dividend yield for stock DE	Find CRM's earnings per share (EPS). Define EPS.	Compare corporate bond yields to municipal bond yields
Create an investment allocation schedule by sector	Define dollar cost averaging	Research taxable vs. non-taxable investments	Find two new investments to create passive income	Identify two alternative investments
Compare mutual funds to ETFs	Define large cap, mid cap and small cap	$ FREE $	Define the wash sale rule	Check fee percentage on employer 401(k) investments
Find the leading company in the Consumer Staples sector	Look up tax rate on long-term capital gains	Research stock symbol VTSAX	Research investing risk levels → determine your risk level	Identify why certain bonds are high risk
Find the current price of gold and why its important	Compare liquid vs. illiquid assets	Look up REITs in Yahoo! Stock Screener	Find out what a hedge fund does	Research two stocks in the Industrial sector

Insurance Page

How are you transferring risk to protect assets?

	Premium	Deductible/ Waiting Period	Coverage
Whole Life			
Term			
Medical			
Disability			
Homeowner's			
Renter's			
Car			
Umbrella			
Long-term Care			

Retirement Page

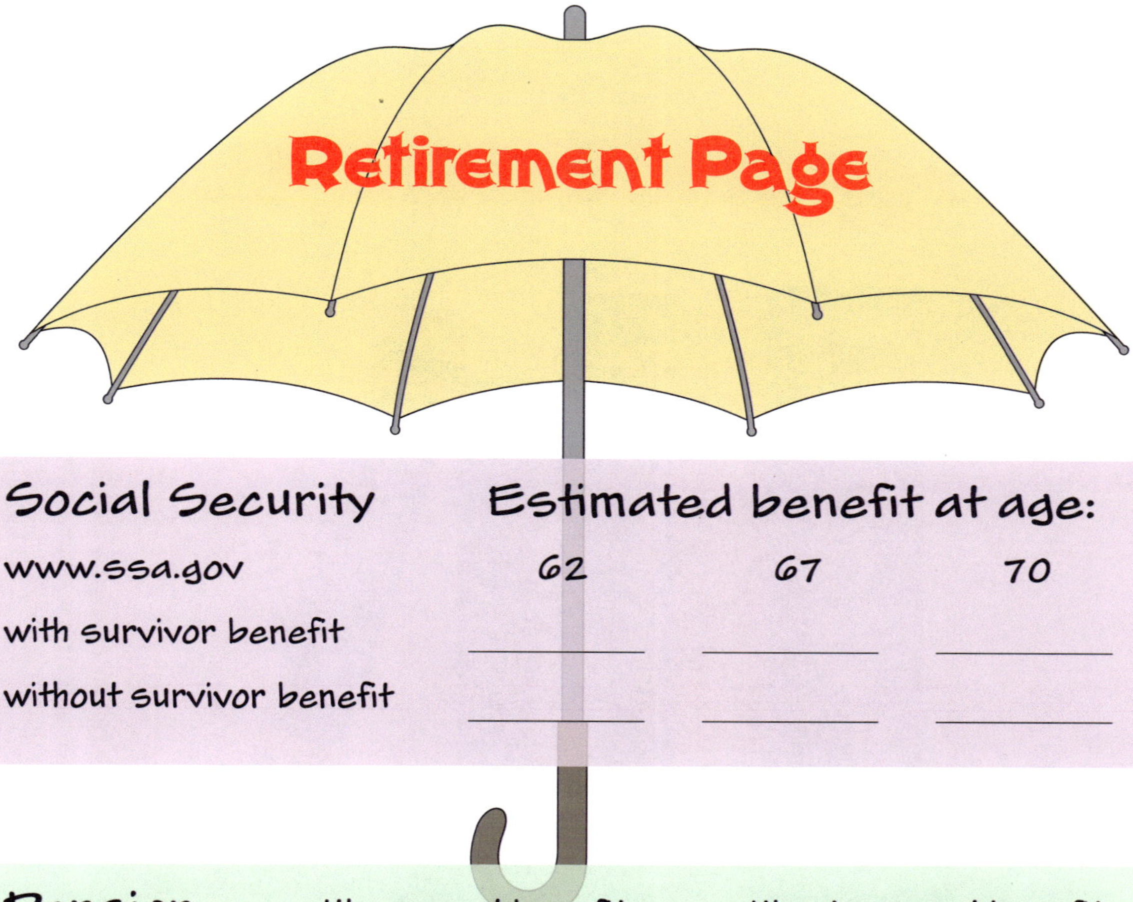

Social Security

www.ssa.gov	Estimated benefit at age: 62	67	70
with survivor benefit	________	________	________
without survivor benefit	________	________	________

Pension

with spousal benefit	without spousal benefit
________	________

Set retirement goals here. What can you contribute to?

Maximum $ ________   ________ % contribution

	Savings	IRAs	401(k) 403(b) 457
Starting Balance:	________	________	________
	________	________	________
	________	________	________
	________	________	________
Total:	________	________	________
Goal:	[ ]	[ ]	[ ]

Suggested Reading List

Notes

Notes

Notes

Made in the USA
Monee, IL
09 November 2026

67972908R00017